Type Tales

Understanding and Celebrating Diversity Through Type

**written and illustrated by
Diane Farris
© 2000**

**Center for Applications of Psychological Type
2815 N.W. 13th Street, Suite 401
Gainesville, Florida 32609**

for Ted and Andrew

TABLE OF CONTENTS

INTRODUCTION AND ACKNOWLEDGMENTS

THE TALES

COMMENTARY

AFTERWORD

REFERENCES

FOOTNOTES

APPENDIX

Introduction and Acknowledgments

These tales descend from stories my grandfather told his grandchildren in a worn green leather chair in Lexington, Kentucky with all the time in the world for stories, poems, songs and conversation. I remember one character called Jojo the dog-eared boy who is no doubt a distant relative of Momo the boy-like dog. I began telling Momo stories to my young son, then to his kindergarten class, then to the other class and so on through the first edition of *Type Tales* in 1991. And now, here is a new edition and the welcome opportunity to revisit the stories, the commentary and the images.

We've all been captivated by story, from the small anecdote that happened on the way here to the evocative "Once upon a time..." As generations of story tellers at firesides, kitchen tables and in classroom corners have always known, there is power in narrative. It can sharpen awareness, deepen understanding, and foster compassion and healing.[1] In recent years, scholars have paid increasing attention to narrative as a way of knowing.[2] Polkinghorn calls it "the primary form by which human experience is made meaningful."[3] As we witness characters weaving their stories, our own unfold into the light.

I experienced memorable evidence of the qualities of narrative when children unexpectedly began requesting Momo stories about important events in their lives: an accident, a divorce, feeling left out. Honored by their solemn confidence, I tried to fashion tales for individuals and groups with particular concerns. When I became interested in how Jungian typology might be helpful to children trying to understand individual and cultural differences, it was a natural step to create more stories and to find Momo a best friend, the redoubtable Millie.

Narrative continued to be important as I moved from teaching to counseling work. Children created narratives with a wide and sometimes wild array of figures and objects in my office sandbox. Most were asked to generate a narrative about the ideal school. Many scripted dreams and movies. Some wrote weekly stories on the computer, and some found their way through difficult personal times by staging elaborate sandbox dramas over months, healing chapters written on paper and in the sand. One preschool boy brought a pouch to his last visit, which he filled with sand to carry home, a reminder of his own healing stories.

These tales of Momo and Millie are offered in hopes that they can expand young people's awareness and acceptance of the different styles they find in themselves and the individuals around them. We can broaden awareness through story and deepen understanding through discussion, example and activities. The hope is that with a deeper knowing of the self and the other, there will be an accompanying interest, identification and compassion.

There are many people I would like to acknowledge and celebrate.

I am grateful to the people of all ages who have shared their stories and reflections with me; they have enriched my life and brought color and texture into this book. I appreciate the people at CAPT, particularly Mary McCaulley and my editor, Keven Ward, and their enthusiastic belief that *Type Tales* should be in print again. It was a gift to revisit the project with new understanding, understanding fostered by valued colleagues whose work is cited in the commentary.

Thanks to Dr. Elizabeth Murphy, Reverend Jeremy Taylor, Dr. Linda Silverman, Dr. Gail Ellison, Mrs. Vera Farris and Ted Runions for their thoughtful readings of the manuscript at various stages, and their invaluable insights.

Thanks are due to the artists who have inspired my photography over the years and those who have recently helped me discover the environmentally-friendly digital darkroom.

Warm gratitude flows always to the friends who speak from the heart when they hold the talking stick and who listen attentively as they pass it along. I am deeply touched by their gifts of time, humor, enthusiasm, wisdom, and courage. Ted Runions, my husband, lights my world with his abiding faith and joyful spirit.

All real living is meeting.
(***Martin Buber***)[4]

The Tales

The Two-Sided Talking Stick

"One year the teacher totally did not know my name," said Momo. He and Millie were walking to school, along the path by the big oak trees. With their golden fur and big ears, Millie and Momo look so much alike they could be twins, but these friends are sometimes very different from each other.

"I don't get that," said Millie. "When the teacher calls your name out, you just say, 'Here!' so she knows she has your name right."

"Well, that's the thing. She had my name *wrong*. She said my middle name by mistake. She just shouted it out in front of everyone on the first day of school."

"Mrs. Jackson doesn't shout."

"Well, it sure sounded loud to me. I was embarrassed," said Momo.

"What *is* your middle name?" asked Millie.

"That's not the point."

"Come on, what is it? We're friends. You can tell me."

"But anytime I tell you something secret, you tell everybody else."

"I'm sorry. I won't tell anyone your middle name. Okay?"

"Okay, so my middle name is. . . .Woodrow."

"Ooh, okay. . . So, why didn't you just say, 'Excuse me, Mrs. Jackson, but I'm called Momo!' Simple. That's what I'd do."

"Well, it's not that simple for me. I tried to say something, but then I felt shy, and I didn't want everyone turning around and looking at me. So I waited until she finished calling out the names."

"Then?" asked Millie.

"Then she went on to tell us other stuff: about the backpack shelf, the lunch line, the library and free time, so I decided to talk with her at lunchtime when no one else was around. . ."

"And?"

"Well, at lunch, I promised myself I would definitely tell her after school."

"So what happened then?"

"I never told her. She called me Woodrow until my parents told her at Parent's Night that my name is Momo."

"Wow. If I have something to say, I just say it. Sometimes I even get in trouble because I don't take time to raise my hand or wait for the teacher to call on me."

"I wish I could speak up like that, right when I want to!" said Momo.

"It's okay, but sometimes I wish I could wait a minute and think about what I'm going to say. Does your class have Talking Stick Circle this year?" asked Millie.

"Yeah, it's great. When you have the stick, you can take your time, and everyone has to wait for you to speak. The stick is cool, too. It's carved with animal heads: a frog, a dolphin and a wolf," said Momo.

"Well, the talking stick may look cool, but I hate to wait

and wait and wait forever for my turn to talk."

"Try listening. It's interesting. Like yesterday, this guy in my class told about catching a striped snake eating an egg in the chicken house at their farm. He took a picture and you could see the shape of the whole egg right in the snake's body."

"Cool—but why bother with a talking stick? Just talk."

"What if someone else keeps talking?"

"If it's me, just interrupt. I don't mind. Is that a new sign? 'Deer Crossing.' There are deer in these woods? All we ever see are noisy squirrels. Yakkety Yak. . ."

"Millie, maybe you need a Listening Stick."

"I *could* use a Listening Stick," laughed Millie. "Want to ride on the new bike trail this weekend?"

Momo looked at the ground as he said, "I'm still learning to ride my bike."

"Come practice with me and my cousins. We fall off all the time, but we just laugh and try again. We'll learn together."

"I'd be too embarrassed. As soon as I learn, though, I want to explore that trail with you," Momo said.

"Okay. Have you started the report on human food yet?" Millie asked, sticking her nose in her lunch bag.

"I went to the library already. I love to read there, because it's quiet. The time went by so fast, I was late meeting my mom. We brought home loads of books and disks. Did you go, Millie?"

"I wanted to, but, for me, the time passes sooo slowly at the library. I keep looking at the clock and taking breaks. Look at all the litter along here. Let's bring a bag tomorrow and pick it up. What was I talking about? Does your family go crazy when you babble in the car and forget what you were talking about?

What does make your parents mad, anyhow?" asked Millie.

"They don't get mad much. They worry when I spend time alone in my room; like last night when I was studying dolphins from this disk I got at the library."

"Oh, yeah, the library! How can I do a good job on the report, Momo?" Millie asked as she waved to some dogs putting up the green school flag.

"Well, let's see, you would rather talk than read and write alone. Why don't you do research with someone else and make up a list of questions and interview people about the food they eat, then write the report together?"

"You mean I could call people on the phone and do my research that way?"

"Sure, it would be really interesting. Just don't ask me to make phone calls."

"Okay, just don't ask me to sit by myself in the library for hours and hours. How come you never phone me?" asked Millie.

"I feel funny about calling. I like it when friends call me, though. That's odd. Maybe I'll phone you tonight."

"Great. The line might be busy, though. I wish I could give the report today," said Millie. "I could just make it up. Sometimes, I raise my hand before I even know what I'm going to say."

"You do? Once I start, I'm okay if I really know what I'm talking about. That's one reason I work hard, so I won't be embarrassed. It's interesting, too. I've already found out that humans eat weird stuff, green stuff, vegetables and fruits that dogs would never eat. I'm illustrating my report. I started with a drawing of grapes."

"I know a dog who eats green grapes, loves them. He'll do tricks for grapes. And tangerines."

"Wow, and I thought we were weird. See you later," said Momo. "Good luck waiting for your turn in the Talking Stick Circle."

"Yeah, right, Woodrow. Meet you at the flagpole after school," replied Millie. The friends laughed as the bell rang, and they hurried into their classrooms.

The Backyard Brontosaurus

Momo and Millie were playing in the backyard when they saw something partly buried in the dirt by the yellow daylilies. Millie looked at it closely but went on searching for the soccer ball. Momo tugged at the thing, but couldn't dig it up. Millie was surprised when he shouted, "We've discovered a dinosaur, Millie, we can have a real archeological dig and—"

"Let me have another look," Millie said. "It's just a plain old bone. Let's practice passing some more. Remember, we're playing soccer on Saturday."

"I'm calling the museum. No, wait, maybe we should dig by ourselves. We have to get those special hats like Indiana Jones and use tools and brushes to dig out the entire skeleton. We've got to be very careful," said Momo as he gently wiped dirt away from the edges of the hard white shape.

"Skeleton?" scoffed Millie. "What skeleton? What are you talking about? It's a boring old bone or maybe even just a rock."

"And then," said Momo dreamily, "we would be famous. Of course, reporters from newspapers and television would come to my house to interview us. They'd want to know how it all

began and how it feels to be so young and already be famous archeologists. You know, not many dogs discover a whole brontosaurus skeleton in their yard and have the skills to deal with it. Where's the camera, Millie? I haven't seen it since my birthday party."

"Momo, the facts are: the brontosaurus did not even live in this part of the world sixty million years ago. We aren't archeologists and, now that I really look at this thing, I'm sure it's a rock. I'm hungry. Let's get a snack and play Scrabble or something. That's what we did yesterday, and it was fun."

"Okay, but I still think—" Momo tripped over a stick because he was walking backwards, looking toward the spot where he thought the dig and the interviews would be. It all seemed so real.

"Momo, honestly, why don't you watch where you're going? You have such a wild imagination. I'll get out the Scrabble, and this time we're using the dictionary."

"Why?"

"Because last time, you made up your own words like 'snorflee' and 'dwull' and got extra points."

"You didn't challenge me on any words," said Momo, licking a peach popsicle.

"I was afraid to. You read so much, I thought you probably knew some really odd words that I never heard of. Why don't we just say you can't make up words at all?" suggested Millie.

"That's part of the fun, inventing new words. Why don't you try it?"

"No, they wouldn't be real words. I don't like it when we have to make up stuff at school, either. I like the teacher to just *tell* me exactly what to do. Let's just do something else."

"We could draw," Momo suggested as he pulled out sketch pads and an old wooden box full of colored pencils and markers.

"Okay," said Millie, picking up a green marker that smelled like limes. "I'm going to draw the big oak trees on the way to school."

"That's a good idea," said Momo, picking up an orange pencil.

"Momo, trees are green, not orange."

"I know that, but I'm going to draw the way the trees make

me feel—safe and happy—and that makes me think of the color orange."

"You know what? Let's build something," said Millie as she dragged the big basket of blocks onto the rug and began carefully stacking some square blocks in the shape of a garage. Momo looked as if he were staring into space, but he was trying to decide which of all his ideas he should build. He decided on a fancy maze with underground passages, large trees, a tower, and maybe even a secret room. His rug was an old green one his great-grandma brought from China, so that could be the grass in the maze. He began lining up blocks to make the wall and then stopped.

"What's wrong?" asked Millie, looking up from the fire station she was building.

"Oh, I've got this idea, but I can never make stuff look the way I see it in my imagination."

"Tell me about your idea, and I'll help," said Millie.

Momo told Millie about the maze: how knights and ladies would explore it with their children and friends, and have adventures and picnics. Maybe a wizard would live in a stone tower and make magic things happen, and there would be a secret garden, and the golden key would be hidden under a mossy stone.

Millie began building, and Momo was excited to see a maze taking shape.

"I am the wizard," said Momo "and I live in this tower with my crystal ball and my ancient books and my super dog. Who are you?"

"Well, I could *pretend* to be something," said Millie carefully. "What could I pretend to be?"

"How about. . . . a dragon?" asked Momo.

"Wow, okay, but remember I'm not really a dragon. I'm only pretending," explained Millie. "You have a good imagination, Momo."

"And you really know how to build things and make them work. We're a good team. Do you think I should wear a tie for the interview?" asked Momo.

"What interview, Momo? What *are* you talking about?"

"With the reporters from the newspaper, when they come about the brontosaurus," Momo explained, patiently.

Millie rolled her eyes and added a curving arch to the doorway of the hidden garden.

The Kind of Fair and Fairly Kind Soccer Game

Saturday, Millie and Momo biked to the park to play soccer. Momo thought how great it was to hang out with friends on a sunny morning and hoped everyone would have a good time, with no arguments. Millie liked to play with friends, too, but she felt annoyed, because there were already two team captains, and she didn't know how they were chosen.

The captains were picking their teams when Momo and Millie ran up. "I want Millie; she's not a great forward, but she's a good fullback," said Angus, one of the captains. "Why don't you take Momo?"

"You know why," whispered Jana, the other captain. Momo wasn't supposed to hear her, but of course he did. "Momo is a really good soccer player, but sometimes he spends so much time cheering everybody up during the game that he doesn't focus on winning."

Momo's feelings were hurt that Jana didn't want him on her team, but he pretended to be looking at an owl way up in a pine tree so no one would notice. Of course he wanted to win, but he did care about his friends' feelings, too. How could you have fun if anyone was sad? He ended up on Jana's team and had to listen to her reminding him to focus on the game. Honestly.

"Millie, I'm sorry Angus hurt your feelings by saying you're not a great forward," he said as they pulled on their shoes.

"My feelings aren't hurt, Momo. He's right. I'm better at fullback. Why would my feelings be hurt when he's just telling the truth?" Millie called over her shoulder as she ran to her position in the grassy field.

It seemed as if the game had just started when a ball zipped past the goalie on Momo's team. Momo thought the goalie, a

dachshund named Dave, looked as if he might cry. Momo ran over to tell Dave that it was okay, that he had really tried hard and that they had plenty of time to have fun and win.

Dave smiled and shouted, "Yeah, Momo, we'll just start fresh and do our best, like you said."

When they took a water break, Millie said there must be a rule about talking to the goalie in the middle of the game. When Momo said "It's only a game," Millie rolled her eyes. When Millie said "The most important thing is to win," Momo rolled his eyes.

He noticed a player from Millie's team who hadn't come in for the water break, and he picked up a bottle to take to her when he went back on the field.

"Momo, I'm sure if Posie wants water, she'll just come get some."

"I'm going right by her; I'll just take her a bottle. Good luck," waved Momo.

As they continued playing, Millie saw someone on the other team, Big Tim, go out of bounds with the ball, but the referee didn't call it. "Great Danes get away with everything," she thought. It was so unfair that she got out of position herself to tell the referee. Angus reminded her that the referee was always right.

"Why is that?" asked Millie.

"It just is," he said. "Get back into position."

"Talk about unfair," she thought to herself.

Millie frowned when Momo reminded her that the referee had a hard job and was doing his best. She did manage to focus on the game again and helped her team win by two goals.

Momo wished she would tell him he'd played a good game, even though his team lost. He said, "Millie, you are a good soccer player."

"Thanks, Momo. I had fun today, except for the referee and Big Tim."

"Yeah, I had fun, too. Millie?"

"Yeah?"

"Do you like playing with me?"

"Of course Momo. It goes without saying. Don't we hang out together all the time?"

The two friends walked their bikes toward their neighborhood, kicking an old blue soccer ball back and forth between them.

The Last Minute Moon

omo heard the phone ringing, but he couldn't find it under the giant pile of baseball cards he'd been looking through.

"What took you so long?" asked Millie.

"You don't want to know. What's up?"

"I finished my homework and wondered if you'd like to play."

"Sure, sounds great!" replied Momo enthusiastically.

"Well, I'm leaving now, so I'll be there in ten minutes. I hope you'll be ready, so we can get organized."

"No problem," said Momo, thinking he should put the phone right back on its stand so the battery wouldn't run down. He put it down beside the fish tank and forgot about it while he sprinkled in some food for the new goldfish. His video games caught his eye, and he decided to play for just a minute. The doorbell rang ten minutes later.

"Momo, you said you'd be ready. What's all this junk everywhere?" As Millie talked, she began straightening up magazines and clothes.

"Stop, Millie! I won't be able to find anything!"

"I was just helping you get organized."

"I *am* organized; I know where everything is, but if you

start moving stuff around, I'll never find it."

"Okay, okay, what's this plane with 'Spir' written on it?"

"That's a model of Lindbergh's airplane, the 'Spirit of St. Louis.' I'm not finished painting it."

"Who's Lindbergh? What's this?"

"He was the first person to fly alone across the Atlantic Ocean without stopping. And that's the Amelia Earhart puzzle."

"I see you're still interested in flying—and really, really old pizza," she said, holding up a disgusting triangle of fuzzy bread.

"That's where that last piece was! It's pineapple pizza from the human food report. You remember."

"Ugh," said Millie, dropping the pizza in the wastebasket. "You know, Momo, I'm different from you about projects. If I begin a model or a book or a puzzle, I like to finish it before I begin the next one."

"Yeah, that's good, too," said Momo. "I guess I just like to have a few things going on at the same time. But sometimes I forget to finish them, and that bothers me. And it really bothers my parents."

"I feel like I have to finish things. If I'm reading a book I don't like, I still finish it. Maybe that's why I don't have as much fun reading as you do."

"If I don't like a book, I begin reading a different one," said Momo.

"Momo," said Millie, looking at the clock by Momo's bed, "how did you know when I'd be here?"

"I just looked at the clock like everyone else," replied Momo.

"But your clock is fifteen minutes fast," said a puzzled Millie.

"Oh, yeah, that's so I can be on time. See, sometimes I'm late because I start doing something and lose track of time, and this way I can kind of fool myself. . . ."

"How can you fool yourself if you're the one who set the clock ahead?"

"I didn't. Mom did. It works for her. How do you get everywhere on time?"

"I just plan ahead. I know how much time it takes to get ready and to get places, and I plan for that."

Momo said, "Ooh, okay. We could work on the maze again. The blocks are still out from the last time we played."

"Okay," said Millie, trying hard not to say that she put her blocks away each time she played with them.

"What's your homework?" asked Momo as they began to build more rooms near the tower, which was quickly becoming a castle.

"A big map of the United States and Canada and Mexico with all the rivers and mountains labeled."

"Wow, I bet you'll be up late tonight," said Momo, "and I bet your parents will be really mad."

"Momo, the map isn't due for two weeks. It's a big project, and that's why I started today. If I do a little every day, it won't be too hard. Besides, I'm working with two other dogs. Why would my parents be mad? What's your homework?"

"Mine's a big project, too. I have to make a model of the moon out of paper maché, paint it and label all the areas."

"When is it supposed to be handed in?"

"Today, but it's all soggy because I just started it last night.

I was trying to dry it with a hair dryer at midnight so I could paint it, but I had to go to bed."

"Do you always do stuff at the last minute?"

"No, not always, but sometimes I can make something really great at the last minute, and it's kind of exciting. I'm upset this time, though, because the moon is late and will get a lower grade. It smells weird, too. I'll begin the next project earlier, that's for sure."

Millie put the wizard and the dragon in the maze and said, "Momo, maybe I'd better go home so you can work. Let's plan something for Saturday after soccer."

"I do want to play on Saturday, but I don't want to plan everything yet. The week is so busy that I like to look forward to some free time on Saturday."

"Okay, but I think it's fun to know what I'm going to be doing. Anyway, one thing we can agree on is that best friends can sure be different from each other."

"That's for sure, Millie. It's so cool that we're friends," said Momo as he walked with Millie to the door.

"See you tomorrow. With your moon. On time," called Millie.

"Of course, I'll just look at my special clock," laughed Momo, waving to his pal.

Commentary

Chapter 1
A Brief Overview of Psychological Type

Narrative knowing fits well with the world of psychological type. Since Isabel Briggs Myers and Katharine Cook Briggs developed a measure grounded in Jung's theories of psychological type, those who have fostered its ethical usage, among them, Dr. Mary McCaulley, have attracted a welcoming community in which all (sixteen) types are valued. It is this inclusive, laterally-structured culture that has allowed the Myers-Briggs Type Indicator measure and philosophy to be embraced across communities as diverse as schools, corporations, and civic and religious organizations throughout the world.

You may be new to or familiar with the concepts of psychological type, but the fact that you have found *Type Tales* indicates an interest in exploring this approach with young people. Our children are living with great change and diversity in their immediate and extended worlds, and type offers one way to make sense of and honor differences.

There is a long-standing tradition of typologies which attempt to systematize and understand human variation. In his 1921 *Psychological Types*,[5] Carl Jung explored three dimensions of orderly differences he had observed over many years in his practice. Tradition has it that one of the reasons for his interest was his attempt to comprehend his misunderstandings with Freud. Katharine Briggs and Isabel Briggs Myers were developing a typology when they came upon Jung's work, for which they had an affinity. They built upon it, writing extensively and developing the MBTI. As it has evolved, psychological type has four dimensions:

- The direction of one's energy: Introversion or Extraversion
- The way one perceives: Intuition or Sensing
- The way one reasons, decides: Feeling or Thinking
- The way one organizes, lifestyle: Perceiving or Judging

The Momo and Millie stories each focus on a dimension of type.

Extraversion and Introversion are the "attitudes" that determine the trajectory of the other dimensions. Extraverted energy goes outward and is replenished while introverted energy is restored within. A central aspect of Extraversion and Introversion has to do with the different ways experience is processed and validated, in company or in solitude. An example might be an extraverted and an introverted individual at the end of a day's work: the individual who preferred extraversion could be ready to reflect on the day in conversation with friends or family and find renewed energy in a social setting, while the person who preferred introversion could desire some quiet time in a tranquil setting to reflect on the day and restore energy in solitude.

Jung called introversion and extraversion the "basic types"[6] and found them to be so universal that he proposed a biological basis for them.[7] While other dimensions manifest later, Jung saw the attitudes appearing as early as a year old.[8]

Intuition, Sensing, Thinking and Feeling are called the functions. Intuition and Sensing are the perceiving functions; they determine what kind of information is foreground for us.

> "Of the two very different kinds of perception, sensing is the direct perception of realities through sight, hearing, touch, taste, and smell....Intuition is the indirect perception of things beyond the reach of the senses, such as meanings, relationships, and possibilities."[9]

Thinking and Feeling are what Jung called the rational functions. They represent distinct cognitive styles and are associated with making choices. Theoretically, a preference for one perceiving or rational function emerges fairly early (by school age, according to von Franz and Hillman),[10] and that preference, or "dominant" as it is called in the literature, becomes a central force in development.[11] This process is often compared to handedness; one hand must assume and develop dominance for the learning of writing and other skills to unfold appropriately, while the other hand provides support and balance. Problems follow if, for some reason, a dominant does not develop.

The dominant function is given part of its character by whether it is extraverted or introverted. Intuitives often are characterized by a richness of ideas and possibilities; in an extraverted intuitive, these ideas would be shared and talked through with others, while in an introverted intuitive, the ideas would characteristically be thought through internally before being broached with others.

The last dimension is one added by Briggs and Myers; it has to do with the way one organizes and plans. The perceiving style is open-ended, comfortable with uncertainty and flexibility. The judging style is more inclined to predictability, planning ahead and closure.

These eight factors combine to create sixteen possible "types." (Please refer to the type descriptions in the Appendix.) The purpose of the approach is not to label individuals, but to foster understanding and awareness through the ideas. Even if one is "typed" with a measure like the MBTI, that is a beginning, not an end in itself. As the reader probably sensed in reading the stories, while we each have all of these aspects within us, some are foreground and some recede. As Dr. McCaulley cautions, there can be as much variation within a type description as between type descriptions. An individual whose type is the same as Millie's could theoretically be as different from Millie as she is from Momo.

What follows is an overview of type that can help shape your discussion and notes.

How are you energized?

With *Extraversion*,
an individual may:

- renew energy by being with others
- process experience in interaction with others
- think out loud
- have many friends
- appear unconcerned about privacy
- learn in public
- laugh at mistakes
- seem impulsive
- appear the same in private and public
- readily share feelings and thoughts`

With *Introversion*,
an individual may:

- renew energy from inside the self
- validate experience internally
- think first, then (perhaps) speak
- need a longer "wait time" to respond
- have a few close friendships
- be very concerned with privacy
- prefer to learn in private
- embarrass easily
- appear reserved
- appear different in public and private
- keep thoughts and feelings inside

What do you pay attention to?

With *Sensing*, an individual may:

- notice the facts
- live in the world of reality
- seek the familiar
- like repetition
- learn in sequential steps, from the beginning
- focus on details
- enjoy the present, what is

With *Intuition*, an individual may:

- think about the possibilities
- sometimes live in the world of imagination
- seek the novel
- be quickly bored with repetition
- learn from various starting points
- focus on the big picture
- enjoy the future, what could be

How do you reason?

With *Thinking*, an individual may:

- use fairness as a guide
- value absolute truth-telling
- hurt feelings without meaning to
- emphasize being right
- think about the rules
- appear to be critical when trying to help
- be solution-oriented

With *Feeling*, an individual may:

- use kindness as a guide
- try to balance truth-telling and others' feelings
- be easily hurt
- value harmony
- think about compassion
- seek something positive while trying to help
- be process-oriented

How do you organize your world?

With *Judgment*, an individual may:

- like to make and carry out a plan
- seek closure, like to finish
- rush decisions
- enjoy one thing at a time
- have a good sense of time, value being on time
- benefit from working with flexibility

With *Perception*, an individual may:

- like flexible plans, open to possibilities
- like beginnings and be challenged by closure
- postpone decision-making
- enjoy many projects simultaneously
- get involved and lose track of time
- benefit from working with organizational skills

Chapter 2

Presenting the Tales to Children

When presenting type to any group, young people or adults, I begin with the ideas. If a measure like the Murphy-Meisgeier Type Indicator for Children (MMTIC) or the Myers-Briggs Type Indicator has been given, the results are saved for later in the session or workshop, when individuals can more easily place them in a context.

Using *Type Tales*, we can simply begin with the stories, reading them while remaining available and interruptible. Remember my grandfather—or yours—in his big, green chair and that sense of having all the time in the world: for stories; for listening; for attending.

It's good to pause to ask who is like this or like that, if this has ever happened to anyone, if the listeners know anyone who appears to feel or behave this way. . . . It is important to mention that we all may sometimes experience each dimension, and that children are still developing preferences. Many children (and adults) have not developed the extreme type preferences expressed by Millie and Momo, so it's helpful both to support exploration and clarify possibilities. Children are often relieved to talk about mixed feelings, feeling or thinking two different ways about something. Such conversation articulates and acknowledges discomfort they may carry as they mull over complex matters in a quick-paced world.

One story at a sitting is probably best, allowing time for questions and discussion. Feel free to customize the stories, editing or expanding as fits. Many presenters gather and share cartoons and other materials that suggest clear type differences in a playful way. *Calvin and Hobbs*, *Sesame Street*, *The Far Side*, *Winnie-the-Pooh* and *Star Trek* are examples of popular resources. One inventive teacher created Millie and Momo puppets to act out the dialogue.

It is helpful to introduce some type language with each story, using the summary overview from the previous chapter. You might, for example, write "Extravert" and "Introvert" on the board after reading the first tale, and list a few of the characteristics. Instances that support the nature of each character are delineated in "Type in the Tales." This list can be drawn upon in discussing the tales later as well.

The pictures are another point of departure for discussion. They can help generate conversation around important aspects of the story, encouraging discussion about matters like games, alone time, sports and imagination. The fact that the dogs look alike helps underscore that we all share all these qualities in different degrees and combinations. Children often project onto the pictures, so an introvert may see the picture of the dog with the phone as Momo avoiding the phone, while the extravert may be sure that it's Millie making yet another call.

As narrative is important in learning, so reflection on the narrative through discussion of the stories is the meaningful next step in bringing the ideas to life.

To know and not to act is not to know.
(Wang Yang-ming)[12]

Type in the Type Tales:
Lists of Characteristics

The Two-Sided Talking Stick:
A Walk with Introverted and Extraverted Energy

Momo's INTROVERSION can be seen in these instances:

- He hesitates to speak in class:
  because he thinks first, sometimes so long that the teacher moves on;
  because he is embarrassed by people looking at him;
  because he doesn't know the teacher well.
- He speaks easily to Millie because he feels comfortable and safe with her.
- He speaks fluently on subjects he knows and cares about.
- He likes to guard his privacy and feels it is very important.
- He can easily listen quietly.
- He needs a longer "wait time" to respond to a question.
- He enjoys blocks of time to read in the library; his work is enhanced by the quiet.
- He does well with a research project.
- He is apprehensive about presenting his report in public and will labor over making it perfect to avoid embarrassment.
- He stays with a topic and likes to explore it in depth.
- He avoids making phone calls, but often enjoys receiving them.
- He treasures the security of this special, close friendship.
- He does quiet activities in the car and in his room.
- He prefers to learn new skills, like riding a bicycle, in private.
- Only those with whom he is comfortable know much about him.
- And— He has a good sense of humor, is a good friend and a loving spirit.

Millie's EXTRAVERSION can be seen in these instances:

- She speaks out:
  thinking as she speaks;
  sometimes impulsively;
  with pleasure;
  without self-consciousness.
- She is not so concerned about privacy, openly sharing things about herself, even with those she doesn't know well.

- She sometimes has difficulty listening, as it can feel like waiting to speak.
- She does not enjoy the quiet part of the library; the time drags and she keeps interrupting herself by taking breaks.
- She does well with an interactive project.
- She is eager to present her project to the class and confident in her ability to "wing it."
- She can be divergent and lose track of the conversation as her attention is attracted to externals, like the deer sign and the litter.
- She doesn't hesitate to make phone calls.
- She doesn't mind learning and making mistakes in front of others.
- She treasures the friendship and has many others as well.
- She sometimes babbles in the car, reading signs out loud.
- Her character is readily seen and understood.
- And— She has a good sense of humor, is a good friend and a loving spirit.

The Backyard Brontosaurus:
Intuition and Sensing Perceptions

Momo's *INTUITION* Preference can be seen in these instances:

- He uses the sensing data as a springboard: a bone becomes a dinosaur.
- His imagination is easily engaged.
- He emphasizes the possibilities.
- He is sometimes not present, but in his imagination, in the past or the future.
- He likes to do new things.
- He likes inventing, as in making up words in Scrabble, thinking of the maze.
- He is not so concerned with the rules in games.
- He is drawn to the possible, the color of a feeling, the new word, the joke.
- He may literally trip over things in the physical world while he's imagining.
- He is drawn to innovation.
- He has a hard time choosing among his many ideas.
- He sometimes has trouble getting started.
- He is discouraged when his efforts don't match what he imagined.
- He can easily pretend to be something or someone else.

- He sometimes daydreams, as he did about the reporters.
- And— He loves to have fun, make jokes and play.

Millie's *SENSING* Preference can be seen in these instances:

- She stays with the sensory data: a bone is a bone; she emphasizes facts.
- She can be uncomfortable with imagining when the parameters are unclear.
- She likes to do familiar activities.
- She is in the present moment.
- She likes to do things the way they were done before.
- She likes to know and abide by "the rules."
- She likes what is "real": the physical color of a tree; a word in the dictionary.
- She is grounded in the physical world, aware of the present surroundings.
- She is drawn to repetition and the sense of mastery it affords.
- Many choices make her anxious; she would rather have a few or a mandate.
- She can easily get started and is inclined to bring projects to closure.
- She can help actualize an idea in the physical world.
- She wants to be very clear about "pretending" and not scare anyone— including herself.
- She can interpret the task at hand too literally, missing the big picture.
- And— She loves to have fun, make jokes and play.

The Kind of Fair and Fairly Kind Soccer Game: Thinking and Feeling Reasoning

Momo's *FEELING* Preference can be seen in these instances:

- Momo is attuned to friends' sensitivities and keeping harmony.
- His feelings are hurt by what the captain says: he hears only the criticism, not that he is a fine player.
- He imagines that Millie's feelings are hurt as his would be.
- He encourages Dave the goalie, which helps Dave play better; they are probably alike in preferring Feeling.
- He knows the rules, but feelings are more important than rules or winning.
- He has empathy for the referee.
- He is upset when someone is unkind.

- He can stretch a truth to save feelings.
- He needs to be affirmed, to hear that others value him.
- He senses that this is perhaps their most difficult difference.
- And— He loves to hang out with his friends on a Saturday.

Millie's *THINKING* Preference can be seen in these instances:
- Millie is bothered by not knowing how the captains were chosen.
- Her feelings are not hurt by what the captain says; she hears both the positive and the negative and keeps them in perspective.
- She is confused when Momo assumes she would be hurt by the truth.
- She doesn't sympathize with Dave; she has a "get on with it" attitude.
- She believes the rules, order, and winning are more important than feelings in the context of the soccer game.
- She is upset when she thinks the referee is unfair.
- She can be critical and think it is for others' "own good," though they may not understand her motivation.
- She thinks that because they are friends, their feelings go without saying. That silence even becomes an indication of how close they are.
- She may not comprehend how difficult this difference is for her friend.
- And— She loves to hang out with her friends on a Saturday.

The Last Minute Moon: Getting Organized

Momo's *PERCEIVING* Preference can be seen in these instances:
- He prefers for free time to be unplanned sometimes.
- He likes the feeling that free time is full of possibilities.
- He sometimes has difficulty carrying through: putting the phone away; being on time; finishing a project.
- He struggles with estimating how long things take, as in thinking he can spend "a couple of minutes" on a video game, or beginning a complicated project the night before it is due.
- He thinks he knows where things are in what appears to be a messy situation.
- He can resent others' efforts to organize him.
- He has several projects and books going on at the same time.
- He sometimes does not complete a project though he is committed to it.
- He is sometimes a better starter than finisher.
- He tends to leave things around on the floor, on the desk, etc., to

remind him of where he left off.

- He tends to leave his plan book at school, perhaps because he is trying to guarantee the free time he values so highly.
- Parents often get irritated with a Momo type for his lack of planning ahead and the consequences to himself and the family.
- He could benefit from time management and organizational skills.
- And— He is eager to work hard, do a good job and please others.

Millie's *JUDGING* Preference can be seen in these instances:

- She finishes her homework before playing.
- She wants to plan their free time.
- She knows and plans for how long it takes to get to Momo's and elsewhere.
- Millie feels a need to organize Momo in a way that is familiar to her.
- She is convinced she can be helpful to him.
- She tends to finish one project before beginning another.
- She stays with a project or a book even if she no longer likes it.
- She likes a clean desk and room so she can get a fresh start each time.
- She tends to get anxious about homework and gets an advance start, sometimes working too much.
- She maintains her plan book and keeps it with her.
- She is frustrated when plans change.
- She may benefit from some help with flexibility.
- And— She is eager to work hard, do a good job and please others.

Chapter 3
Type Dynamics
of the Characters

Many sources offer informative descriptions of each of the sixteen types.[13] In the Appendix is an annotated type description to help place our two dogs, and other characters you may have in mind, in the perspective of the full range of types. Below are two extensive type descriptions for those opposite individuals, Millie and Momo. The descriptions are taken from my counseling work with children and offer the reader a sense of how type dynamics can be helpful to those trying to understand a child, encourage and enhance his or her strengths and work gently and non-judgmentally with challenges. The descriptions are presented much as I would share them with families, so there is some repetition of details such as the Thinking–Feeling distribution data.

Characteristics of each dimension have been explored in the tales and listed in Chapter II, but these attributes don't actually occur in isolation. They are like dance steps that find their full meaning only as they come together and are enlivened by music. We can describe some of the characteristics of a person who prefers Feeling, for example, but introverted and extraverted Feeling look very different, as Feeling combined with Sensing lives out differently from Feeling combined with Intuition. Some combinations of factors potentiate each other, and some can create balance or tension in the internal dynamic.

In the sample descriptions of an ESTJ (Millie) and an INFP (Momo), some of the dynamics among the factors are discussed. A few suggestions will be offered on how each of these youngsters might learn best and how to address less developed skills. Isabel Briggs Myers stressed that children need to develop their strong preferences first in order to meet the world, process information and make decisions.[14] Toward the end of each description, a paragraph on the Ideal School exercise is included to illustrate how children of different types respond to the suggestion that they imagine the perfect school. These are taken from children's responses to this invitation and give a glimpse into school culture from different individuals' perspectives. As noted earlier, young children often do not indicate a strong preference on one or more of the dimensions, so Millie and Momo would be unusual in their clarity and intensity of preference, but they highlight some of the strengths and challenges of certain aspects of type.

Millie, who is, among other things in life, an "ESTJ"

Millie's type is Extraverted, Sensing, Thinking and Judging. While many young people have some strong and some mild or unclear preferences, Millie's score was clear on each of the dimensions. The combination of factors work together in some interesting ways.

Her dominant way in the world is Extraverted Thinking. She knows her opinions, feels confident they are correct, and readily shares them. Millie has a clear vision of how the world should be and finds it difficult not only to entertain another position, but to entertain the thought that there might *be* another position.

As one with a preference for Thinking, Millie is very concerned with fairness and can get hung up if she doesn't know:

- why something is being done, such as a lesson being presented;
- how a decision has been made, such as the choosing of captains;
- the rules and whether everyone is abiding by them;
- what is going on when something seems unfair.

As an extravert, Millie is energized by interaction. She probably has abundant energy at the end of a school day or any active day and may sometimes even seem overextended or "hyper" with too much stimulation. She also may need to talk experiences through to better comprehend and integrate them.

As someone with a preference for sensing, Millie is concerned with what is "real," the facts. Combining that with thinking and judging preferences, she is someone who can decide what to do and get it done, but she may miss out on the "big picture" and may be overly hasty in wrapping something up that could productively be given more consideration. Millie's sensing is manifest in her comfort in repeating favorite activities with known parameters, staying with the rules, and needing clarity around "pretending."

Millie attests that reading is not her favorite activity, partly because she reads slowly and deliberately and finishes even books she doesn't like. She indicates that she prefers factual books about nature, science and biography. She also mentions that she enjoys reading or listening to favorite books over and over.

Millie is a lot of fun and loves to joke and play, but she likes some of the same clear rules and boundaries in play that she wants in the rest of her life. If she's not careful, other children (and adults!) can see her as not only competent, but bossy. Sometimes, Millie's jokes are sarcastic and can be unintentionally hurtful. Her certainty and self-confidence can be intimidating to some. She said that she is trying to learn to listen, something about a "listening stick." Millie could become an excellent leader as she matures if her empathy and compassion are cultivated.

The third dimension of type is Thinking–Feeling and has to do with how people reason and make decisions. An individual who prefers Thinking uses logic and fairness to make decisions while a person with a Feeling preference uses feelings, empathy and kindness in that process. The world is probably experienced quite differently by Feeling and Thinking types, and it is easy for them to misunderstand and hurt one another. This is the only dimension on which there is a sex difference. There are more male thinkers and more female feelers (approximately 65%–35%), so there is a cultural factor if one goes "against stereotype" as Millie does. Throughout her life, she may have to cope with being admonished to be "more feminine."

As a dominant thinking type, Millie values logic and fairness in making decisions and expects others to do the same. In the family, it would be helpful for others to remember to explain decisions from this perspective so she will be more comfortable and cooperative. The language of logic can be helpful in communicating with her: e.g., "The weather changed, so it made sense to postpone the drive, because it wasn't safe and we couldn't see the animals we were going to see."

Another way that Millie's thinking preference is seen is in her level-headed assessment of her own strengths and weaknesses. The other side of this is that she can be oblivious to the self-esteem struggles and affection needs of the dominant feeling type of individual. Elizabeth Murphy describes Thinking self-esteem as a mountain with positive and negative experiences adding or subtracting a cupful of dirt. She describes Feeling self-esteem as a balloon, with life's experiences either making it buoyant or totally deflated.[15]

The last dimension has to do with preference for traditional organization versus need for flexibility. People who enjoy planning, being on time, starting with a clean desk, and finishing projects have the unfortunately-named preference, Judging. In this context, a judging style indicates a preference for order, planning, closure, etc. Though most children prefer the more spontaneous perceiving style, Millie is a strong judging type in her planning, organizing, being concerned with time and finishing projects (even if she is no longer committed to them), with plenty of energy left over to organize others.

The ESTJ child can easily be derailed by a change of plans or feel a parent has "lied" when things aren't exactly as he or she thought they would be. So, it is good to get in the habit of articulating and clarifying: "This is the plan at this time; We think the day will be like this, but this time is open; This plan could change..." etc. As one of the certainties in life is change, her family would do well to cultivate spontaneity and flexibility in the family—not radically, but in small ways. It might be fun to have an hour each week, "Surreal Thursdays from Three to Four," for example, where something unexpected will happen; the sensing children can get excited about this, partly because of the safety of the time boundary.

Millie was asked what the Ideal School would be like and was told that she could invent everything about it. She seemed confused by the notion and talked about the school she goes to, including a lot she doesn't like about it. She was very concrete about what school is (exactly like the school she attends!) and somewhat apprehensive (as she is in pretending). I asked her what would make sense and be logical in organizing a school, trying to use words that she might find more comfortable. (Often individuals of Millie's type are allergic to "brain-storming" if it's broached as a totally open-ended enterprise.)

Finally, she said that there would be a "manual" for the school that lays out how everything is to be. The teachers would be clear and tell kids why they are studying certain topics. The teachers would be experts in their subjects. There would be more science and math and more time with computers. You wouldn't have to go to art, but if you went, you would learn how to draw "real things." She wasn't comfortable imagining different foods or playground activities. Her type shows itself here as she tends toward the concrete and logical, insisting at first that she doesn't understand the suggestion, but then moving some with encouragement because she does, after all, have good ideas on how things are supposed to be.

Otto Kroeger's catch phrase for the ESTJ is "Life's Administrator."[16]

Momo, who is, among many other things in life, an "INFP"

Momo's type is Introverted, Intuitive, Feeling and Perceiving. While many young people have some strong and some mild or undecided preferences, Momo's preference scores were clear on each of the dimensions, and they work together in some interesting ways.

His dominant function is Introverted Feeling. He makes his decisions with feeling, kindness and compassion. What the world sees is his Intuition, his love of imagination and possibility. People, including family members, may be surprised at how decisive he is when he manifests his introverted dominant feeling preference. This could happen either when he feels very comfortable or when some deeply held value is challenged and he must rise to its defense, even risking embarrassment, a big issue for many introverts. He needs time to reflect in order to comprehend and integrate his experiences.

Momo's introversion can be seen clearly in his thinking before he speaks. He often doesn't speak at all in public situations, partly because he is reflecting deeply and takes too long for many situations such as a classroom, and partly because of his fear of embarrassment, so that he may get into a cycle of "Maybe if I thought about it more, practiced it more. . . ." Family and teachers need to help him out of this cycle; it can lead to a paralyzing perfectionism so that he tries too hard or doesn't dare to risk at all. He misses the opportunities to practice articulating his thoughts and, each time, the stakes are subtly higher and he is more reluctant, though he has much of value to share.

It's evident that Momo appears extraverted with his closest friends and family; they could help him by drawing out his ideas and facilitate his practicing a quicker response. It will also help to boost his confidence in his ideas and thinking as he sometimes feels "weird" with his colorful imaginings. His confidence will be strengthened not with praise (which he distrusts), but with genuine attention—asking questions and making the kinds of observations that indicate engaged listening. An individual with a preference for Feeling needs to know explicitly that he or she is valued.

While people with a preference for Thinking can learn from anyone who is knowledgeable, those with a preference for feeling often need to feel a mutual regard with a teacher in order to learn. As the Feeling person matures, he/she can consciously decide to learn in a wide variety of situations.

Momo's preference for Intuition helps him generate an abundance of interesting ideas. It is painful to select one project to work on, partly because that eliminates the other potential projects. This tendency is furthered by his preference for Perceiving, which makes him desire to keep all the exciting options open as long as possible. Thus, he can end up choosing late and under duress, doing a last-minute job that does not satisfy him. This embarrasses him and displeases those whose esteem he seeks and values.

Family and teachers can be very helpful in assisting his early explorations of the possibilities, then helping him decide and develop a realistic time line with concrete visual aids to ground him. It's good to use language he values, such as having time to work "in depth," do "quality" work, feel "proud" of it and "please" others and himself.

Momo says he enjoys reading, that he likes fiction and fantasy as well as explorations of topics of curiosity like dinosaurs and astronomy. Momo can sometimes be "all over the place" in his interests; again, it is helpful to point out his own inclinations: "I see you got another book about marine biology; that's been a continuing interest. Tell me about it..."

On the last dimension, Momo preferred Perceiving, as do most children. People with a preference for keeping things open, seeing what comes up, beginnings rather than closures are called Perceiving types. Note that they are not necessarily disorganized; they organize differently. Thus the Perceiving child with piles of baseball cards, clothes and Nintendo games all over his floor probably knows where things are and may be upset if a well-meaning judging type "cleans up," as was Momo when Millie tried to "help."

Some of the suggestions for organization of projects address this tendency. Also, Momo is "global" in his perceptions, so when a parent says, "Clean up your room," the instruction is often an invitation to disaster, or at least divergence. The task can be broken down into small parts such as, "Put all the clothes that are touching the floor in the hamper and come back for your next instruction." Momo may be so involved with his imagination that it might work to write the instruction on a card and have him hand it in for another card, a smile and a hug. This needs to be fun, remember, and kind.

Momo would say he was embarrassed when his (excellent) report card was posted on the refrigerator. It made him anxious that he would have to get on the honor roll again the next grading period, and he worried each time he saw it. It might be enough just to ask his permission to put it up so that his sense of privacy is honored. He'll probably say yes, if asked.

But he'll never say yes to having his parents talk about what he considers private (that would be almost everything) about his life on the phone and with their friends and relatives. He needs to know that his parents understand this, even though they may be different. His friend Millie certainly is different, and they are trying to work that out.

It's clear that introverts may easily feel embarrassed. They can learn to ride a bike or hit a baseball, but it needs to be practiced in private first. They often wither with the teacher who corrects children in front of the class or who uses sarcasm. If he needs correction, then private correction will be more effective. While he needs very much to become his own advocate—partly so he can get the practice in speaking that his extraverted peers get continuously—someone needs to be aware of the atmosphere of his classroom and advocate on his behalf if necessary.

Thinking–Feeling is the only dimension on which there is a gender difference. There are more male Thinking types and more female Feeling types, so there is a cultural factor if one goes "against stereotype." Momo quoted his dad as saying that "big guys don't cry," and this is something to ponder. He needs to know that his sensitivity is valued, and he also needs to develop strength. Among very bright children, there are many males with a preference for Feeling whose compassion is a fine asset.

Momo is a good friend and is deeply attached to a few friends and family members, as are most introverts. Be aware that if any of his close circle move away, it will be extremely difficult. It is worth helping him maintain contact with distant friends through email, mail, calls and/or visits.

The Intuitive Perceiving person learns best with rich ideas and innovative presentation. Momo does not like or learn optimally from repetition. If he can do the first three answers on a math sheet, he probably has grasped the concept and to continue to drill would be counterproductive. Children like Momo have actually stopped doing worksheets (which is very rebellious for this type that loves to please) because the repetition seemed so futile and insulting. I've asked what happens when they finish such a sheet, and they've said that they are handed another one. Their solution? Don't finish. Perhaps it would help if they have different work available, a research project or a book that they can work on once they've demonstrated mastery of a concept. Then, the dreaded "show your work" can be the key to treasured freedom of choice.

When asked to design the Ideal School, Momo immediately named it, "The Amazing School." He had often commented on the disappointment of school and was gleeful (and remarkably extraverted) as he imagined:

"It would be in the city, but there would be a field for sports and a field for animals because the school would have lots of pets like turtles and goats and horses. All the grades would be mixed so that friends could be together. There would be lots of choices and students could decide what to do. You could stay in art all day, or move around to different things. Of course you have to learn certain things.

"The teachers would be really nice and love children. They would laugh a lot and have really fun ideas. They would listen to kids and have time.

"There would be all kinds of food in the lunchroom, mostly vegetarian, but really good, like pizza. You could bring your lunch and trade stuff if you wanted to.

"In gym, you could swim or play basketball, volleyball, baseball, frisbee, all kinds of sports. Everyone would get to play and feel good. Sometimes they wouldn't even keep score.

"Music would not be boring. You could play drums and guitars and learn other instruments. There would be an art studio where you could work with clay and paint. There would be supplies to do whatever project you wanted to. You could do all kinds of experiments in the science lab, but you would have to be safe.

"The students would help people like refugees and homeless people and Save the Dolphins.

"The grades would be on how much fun you had and how much you learned and if you were nice to other people. Kids would help each other and other people. You would get a note sent home if you were yelling at people and didn't make any jokes."

The Amazing School is full of possibility, but has its structure; there are adults, and there is meaningful content to be mastered. The library, science lab and art room are richly stocked for learning. The style is definitely Intuitive and Feeling. There is a range and variety of choices. Ideas are valued. Repetition is minimal. Friends are together; teachers like children; there are pets to love; games aren't scored; and people don't yell in conflict.

Kroeger's catch phrase for the INFP is "Performing Noble Service and to Aid Society." [17]

Chapter 4
Some Notes on Families

It can be enjoyable and productive to reflect on a family culture from a type perspective. As always, the goal is to deepen awareness, understanding and compassion, not to categorize or criticize. From the stories, notes and references, it should be possible for every family member to get a sense of his or her type inclinations. A type map that includes grandparents and other relatives charts an intriguing landscape. Just looking at such a map, people have understood the attraction or antipathy between family members in extended families. One woman noted with shock that all the "outsiders" in her intellectual family were the individuals with a preference for Sensing–Perceiving and that her delightful Sensing and Perceiving child was beginning to be marginalized at big family gatherings.

It is important to discuss ways we are alike as well as ways we are different and to maintain a constant awareness that everyone in the family cherishes the same deep, important values: wanting to share love and respect and be engaged in meaningful activity.

In the early data gathered on type,[18] it was proposed that the North American character is Extraverted, Sensing, Thinking and Judging, like Millie in the tales. This fits with early stereotypes of U.S. citizens as doers and pioneers. In Myers' data, Millie's type appeared to be the prominent national character, and Momo's, the polar opposite, appeared to be rather rare. Recent data[19] indicate that the pattern probably still holds, but that the split may not be as profound. Millie's type is one of the two most frequent at 10-12%, and Momo's among the rarest at 4–5%.

From the discussions above, it is clear that introverted and extraverted people have some similar and some different needs in families. Mary Sheedy Kurcinka offers a good discussion of Introversion and Extraversion in children in her *Raising Your Spirited Child*.

The introverts in the family may need more down time to gather their resources. They may prefer some quiet at the end of a busy day or on a car trip. They may be sensitive to admonishments to get out and play, call someone, etc. when they are drawn to solitude.

They often have a complicated relationship to praise. As do other types, introverted individuals thrive on appreciation, but they are finely tuned to the fit between the appreciation and what they feel they have actually accomplished. We live in a time where many believe that any praise will automatically raise self-esteem. If there are accolades for doing something one doesn't value, something that came too easily, that one already knew or didn't do up to one's ability (though the grade may be an A or the score lofty), self-esteem actually suffers, in both extraverts and introverts. Myers emphasizes earning satisfaction:

> "Both home and school should provide them with the experience of doing particular things well and thereby earning the satisfaction they crave. Because the various types have different gifts and needs, the specific things and satisfactions cannot be the same for all children. . .To promote development, schools should not disregard excellence, but diversify its recognition by rewarding non-academic excellences as well. . ." [20]

As has been highlighted with Momo, the introvert often recoils from public recognition like the report card on the refrigerator, the conversation with the parents' friends, the bumper sticker declaring, "My child is an honor student at..." On the other hand, students might be happy to have work displayed, but the invitation is important: "I'd like to display your work—is that all right with you?" The request itself assures the individual that he or she is being respected and has some control.

Many introverted individuals expect to be and are pained by being misunderstood. Active listening enriches all relationships. Good listening can be intuitive, but it seems an increasingly rare skill. There are excellent resources: Hendrix[21] gives clear guidance on active listening skills which he calls "intentional dialogue," as do the older books by Haim Ginot.[22] Dinkmeier's *Encouragement Book* is a resource for ideas for keeping a supportive conversation going without raising the stakes too high. For example, instead of posting a good science grade and proclaiming, "You are a great scientist. Watch out Einstein!" some alternatives might be: "I'm intrigued with your science topic—it's something that's always interested me, too." Or, "You spent a lot of time researching this." Or, "You seem really interested in this topic...."

Another major complaint that many introverted children air about parents is the sharing of information about them, virtually any information. A typical scenario might be a mother talking to a friend or relative about a child's performance in a play, work in school or meeting with a friend. Introverts usually have a strong need for privacy and when asked what is private, they often answer "Everything!" It is sometimes a revelation to an introvert that one can actually talk about these matters with extraverts/adults/authority figures, and be heard. This takes some coaching, but can be life-altering.

This is not to say that introverted people don't like to talk about what is important. They usually thrive on authentic conversation, but it needs to be thoughtful, not on-the-run or about them to a third party. However, people with a preference for Introversion can be so intense within themselves that the casual conversation in the car, on a walk to feed some ducks or while having a meal together may be preferred settings for comfortable conversation.

I've found that sometimes just being quiet with an introvert or affirming, "Sometimes it's hard to talk" or "You may not feel much like talking" can get the conversation going. After such a low-key opener, it's important to wait, often longer than many of us are comfortable pausing. I've observed pairs of extraverted parent/introverted child interactions, and it can be like watching a painful film clip in slow motion; just as the child is about to act or draw or speak, the parent seems to swoop in and take over, sensing—erroneously, but understandably—that the child is never going to respond.

A note about this apparent complexity. Theoretically, the introverted person's dominant function is internalized, so we are used to seeing his/her second strongest preference or auxiliary function. In the case of Momo, he meets the world as an intuitive, but his dominant preference is Feeling. Millie meets the world with her dominant, Thinking, thus the sense that with her, "What you see is what you get." There is some truth to the impression. If Millie and Momo were both working on a save-the-wildlife campaign, for example, we might expect Momo to generate many excellent ideas for the campaign and Millie to logistically engineer it. What could surprise us is Momo's deep passion for the cause, strong conviction which might not be evident on the surface.

Another interesting dynamic can occur between the introverted parent and the extraverted child. One scenario is the child pressing the parent for a decision while the parent needs time to reflect. One parent offers in such instances: "If I decide quickly, you may not like my decision; come back in an hour, and we'll talk about it." The time could vary; the important thing is conveying what it takes for the individual to make a good decision, and understanding that pressure not only isn't helping, but could be counter-productive. Again, type language can be helpful: "I need time to make a solid/creative/fair/kind decision."

We'll touch on the concept of the shadow in the notes on counseling, but its presence may be manifesting in a fairly common dynamic with introverted children. Sometimes parents hear how beautifully-mannered their children are at school and in other settings, while witnessing their rage at home. This has been noted by Silverman in her work with intellectually gifted children.[23] Some of the explanation may have to do with the frustration the introverted child can experience at school where the day can move in a fast-paced, fragmented way, coupled with the safety they feel in letting go at home. When behavior is extreme, a close look needs to be taken at the child's life, especially the school life, if things are harmonious at home. One parent changed her child to a different school when she was appalled to hear herself saying to him, mid-tantrum, "Of course you're miserable at school. . . ." She decided that there was nothing natural about his misery, and the change of school returned her contented, curious child to the family.

The extraverted child presents a different dynamic. While we are often trying to get the introvert out of her room, we are sometimes trying to get the extravert into his. Both efforts may be less important than we think. The child with a preference for Extraversion may well study better near us in the kitchen, may learn through talking or in partnership with another (serious, carefully chosen) student. While we become accustomed to attributing complexity to the introvert for some of the reasons discussed above, we can usually accept what the extravert is presenting to us as foreground interests and concerns. Communication skills such as active listening are equally critical with the extraverted child. While our mirroring conversation with the introvert will help draw out his/her concerns, the same kind of conversation with the extravert will help focus and clarify his/hers.

The extraverted child can move into what we've called the "babbling" mode. Sometimes a parent will pull away from this, but the opposite, full attention, can be helpful and get to the heart of the matter. After grasping what is being said, the parent can respond, address the situation, or say he needs some quiet but will talk at a specified time. As Millie suggests, extraverts are sometimes interruptible. When I taught, I kept tape recorders on hand for extraverted students who needed to talk through an idea but couldn't find a partner at the time. Many took advantage of the opportunity to think out loud, especially when affirmed that this was a good way to think.

While riding in a car, extraverts and introverts can make good-natured contracts to alternate quiet and talking time. Extraverts can have a tape recorder with earphones to listen to talking books or music during the quiet time if they like. It's preferable to get this issue out on the table before a trip rather than have a lot of stress and discomfort on the road. Again, the attitude is one of celebration of differences and creative problem-solving to find the optimal situation for everyone.

As in the stories, the Thinking–Feeling difference can generate misunderstanding and hurt. I've seen this poignantly portrayed in couples, and also in parent-child interaction. The most familiar scenario is the sensitive wife who prefers Feeling paired with a matter-of-fact husband who prefers Thinking; she needs more overt affirmation that she is loved and valued, and he needs her to understand that his marrying her was the ultimate statement of love and value. Clearly, they must find a way of speaking one another's language so they can enjoy what they share. Again, Hendrix's work is an excellent resource.

In the stories, there is the male who prefers Feeling and the female who prefers Thinking, both going against persistent cultural stereotypes. When such a boy has a father with crystal clear conceptions of what a man is like, there can be serious problems as the feeling child strives to please, overriding his own wisdom and sensitivities. The earlier family members can learn to actively listen to one another and honestly value differences while celebrating their shared love, the better and the more positive future for all concerned. Some of the most alienated adolescents I've encountered have been children who prefer Feeling in families characterized by Thinking values; these young people often were reacting to their parents' disappointment in not having a child like themselves. Such a young person is at risk, of course, and we all suffer the loss of their unfulfilled talents and gifts.

What we are dealing with in the above case has been referred to as "falsification of type," and perhaps children with a Feeling preference who strive to please parents with the opposite preference are especially vulnerable to it. They pay a high price. Instead of developing their own clear way of encountering the world, they develop a weak version of someone else's, which may further irritate the parent looking for a particular kind of strength. The literature describes this situation as ranging anywhere from uncomfortable to profoundly damaging. It makes sense that the child struggling with this process feels weak and uncentered and may be missing critical developmental milestones that cannot be readily recovered.

While Thinking and Feeling preference conflicts can go deep in relationships, it is often the organizational differences that counselors hear about from families. Family members can be very critical of one another's: laxity or obsessiveness about time; procrastination or planning; messiness or neatness. Thinking in type terms can take some of the critical judgment out of negotiations around these issues and pave the way for helpful time-management and flexibility coaching.

As has been noted, it is helpful in families to speak some of the language of people of different types, consciously including factual and concrete references for the sensor, for example, and images of possibility for the intuitive. An extraordinary speaker once told me that he included something for every type dimension in his talks, making a special effort to be sure that he had included at least a few words that would have significance for those different from himself.

A fascinating series of films called *The Way of the Dream* focuses on the thought of Jung's associate, Maria von Franz. At one point, she was asked "What are parents to do?" She appeared almost puzzled at the question and replied to the effect that parents have the same task as all people, consciously developing their own awareness and maturation, in the process Jung called "individuation."

Chapter 5

Some Notes on Education

If teachers are thinking that here's yet another course of knowledge to add to an already crowded menu, be assured this is not the case. It is for many teachers a great help to get a feel for type differences and a sense of how one's own type preferences shape the culture of the classroom. It can make classroom life easier and more comprehensible, enhance lesson planning and free time.

If I had to select one concrete suggestion for teachers, it would be to add a few seconds of wait time after all questions. Myers reports on data from the mid–'70s[24] documenting that teachers habitually waited one second after asking a question before speaking to pose another question, repeat the same question or move on to another student. When teachers increased wait time to only three seconds, the number and quality of responses increased dramatically; the perception of the previously "least promising" students also improved significantly.

The introvert is disadvantaged by the one-second custom, not just for the moment, but cumulatively over the years as he or she has less and less experience and practice with speaking, sometimes becoming increasingly discouraged and inward. What Myers brings out as well is that while the introverted student needs time to decide what she or he will say, the sensing student needs time to go over what was just said. For extraverted teachers in crowded classrooms with time constraints, three seconds can seem like a long time. They may have to practice with a second hand at first. But the profound academic and personal benefits are well worth the extra few seconds.

A teacher might be overwhelmed by the thought of differentiating lessons for different types of students, but the task actually is to help the students know their own strengths and ways to differentiate learning *for themselves*. Once an extraverted student understands his/her strengths, he or she doesn't give up on a task like researching a report, but can learn to find ways to make it work and work well. The goal of learning a specific body of information isn't altered, but the way it is approached can be tailored. The teacher can offer options that appeal to the different preferences. The *Type Tales* themselves provide a unit which should begin to help children and young people become attuned to their personal strengths and challenges.

In reflecting on one's classroom and teaching, it is helpful simply to become aware of one's own preferences and the opposites. Murphy[25] has done numerous experiments with teachers, sorting them by sensing and intuitive functions and by dominant preference. In one experiment, sensing and intuitive teachers created lessons to teach vocabulary. While students with a sensing preference found the sensing lessons satisfactory, students with an intuitive preference found them boring. On the other hand, sensing students found the intuitive lessons confusing, while intuitive students were off and running with them.

In another of Murphy's experiments, teachers with different dominant functions were asked to design exam questions around a unit on drugs. Teachers who preferred Sensing focused on the facts. Teachers who preferred Intuition asked for essay questions. Teachers with a preference for Thinking targeted cause and results. Teachers with a preference for Feeling focused on how drug use affects people. Murphy's suggestion is that teachers team up with others to see how their units and exams are received by individuals of different types. As in the case of the speaker mentioned earlier, sometimes it is enough to include language that has significance for people of other preferences. Such an effort signals, "The teacher is speaking to me."

One delightful way to introduce school faculty and administration to type ideas in a meeting or short workshop is to do a reading of *I Am a Good Teacher,* a play by Elizabeth Murphy.[26] In it, she highlights each function—Intuition, Sensing, Thinking and Feeling—by having a teacher talk about lessons and students from the perspective of that function. Then, there are responses from "students" with each preference. In a playful way, personal and classroom dynamics become clarified.

An example of lesson planning with type is a unit on the game of chess for elementary school students. Chess is inherently intuitive and thinking, as it demands logical strategies and projecting imagination several moves into the future. I wanted to involve more individuals than those who naturally gravitate to the game, and thinking about type was helpful. As we discussed how the pieces moved, students were invited to create stories about them, including their motivations. One girl wrote that the "king is fat and the queen is fit," which helped her remember that the king could only move one square in any direction, and the more aerobically fit queen could traverse the entire board in a number of ways. The class designed a chess set and carved rubber stamps from their drawings, so that each person could have a set. The task of creating and building the sets so that they would last, stand up and actually be used was an engaging sensing and intuitive problem. One side had the traditional horse for a knight; the other side had a magical person leaping from cloud to cloud in the knight's dog-leg pattern. One side had a fortress-like castle and the other, a homey castle. One side had little warrior pawns and the other, strong female troops. As this unit unfolded, everyone learned the game and, for those who already knew it, understanding was enriched by the many perspectives that came into play.

An example of tailoring a project to an individual comes from a third grade student I once taught. This was a child who was very discouraged with the first four years of school because she had learned very little about her life goal of becoming a physician on a space station. She had completed an extensive independent research project on bacteria. She felt it was important to share her discoveries with the whole elementary school, but was extremely shy. We brain-stormed possibilities and decided to make a videotape of a puppet show that she would create and perform; thus she would never have to directly appear or address a group, but she could still share her research. The goal was to learn and share a body of information, but the ways of doing that were unlimited and could be tailored to this student's strengths. As we, then she alone, traveled from class to class with the videotape, she gradually began to introduce it, field questions and enjoy the process—an unexpected and welcome bonus.

Another introverted student told me that everyone was required to be in the class play wearing what he thought were embarrassing outfits. We thought of a number of other jobs that he would be willing to do—costuming, prompting, video, lights, programs—and asked his parents to help him present them to the teacher, for whom this was a new and apparently welcome approach. The teacher viewed the play experience as educationally important and had at first seen this student as rebellious. She was open to the meeting, which had a good outcome for everyone.

Coaching can be invaluable in reaching a "win-win" situation. It poses the intriguing question: "How can one accomplish what is required or desired and honor who one is?" The coach, often the teacher or parent, comes to the encounter with confidence that this can be done and that the process will be interesting, worthwhile and affirming.

Introversion once again surfaces as a particular area of concern. Sometimes the culture and the classroom do not promote the introvert's growth and sense of worth. As Wickes wrote in 1927: "Since our Western civilization is essentially extraverted we are in danger of undervaluing the introverted child. He needs more reassurance in his contacts with life." [27] Some literature indicates that introverts are prominent in the intellectually gifted population.[28] Taken from a two-year sample of my counseling practice, 90% of the gifted students I saw were intuitive feeling types, 70% of whom were introverts. As this was a counseling setting, the data may simply indicate that bright young people with preferences for Introversion and Feeling seek or are brought to counseling more frequently than others. My sense was that this group was having a particularly difficult time with the society, school, peer and family culture, feeling outside and longing to belong, but in ways consistent with their closely held values. Linda Silverman's observations indicate that the higher an individual's IQ, the more likely he or she is to be introverted. She sees such individuals as increasingly vulnerable to isolation and depression.[29]

In a survey I conducted in 1987–88 in an elementary school, a clear pattern that emerged was that the gifted students were more decisive about their preferences. Of the regular classroom population, 38% had scores in the "undecided" area of the MMTIC while only 22% of those in gifted classes had scores in the "u-band." This earlier formation of ways to take in, reason and make decisions about information could enhance development in many aspects of life, including academics. About 50% of this group was intuitive feeling perceiving or intuitive thinking perceiving as opposed to 30% of the regular classroom students. This finding is consistent with Williams' work in Texas in 1992 which found 58% of her gifted sample to prefer Intuition and Perceiving as opposed to 23% of the general population.

In addition to coaching introverts in private and allowing ample time for them to answer, I've found pairing introverts with other introverts in projects is an excellent way to give them practice speaking. Suddenly, their area of the room becomes very lively, as they share deeply considered ideas with one another. The more traditional pairing of an introvert with an extravert often results in the extravert taking over and the introvert falling silent, missing the very practice in articulating and negotiating that they need. Extraverts paired with one another, too, must find ways to negotiate listening and talking, essential learning for them.

In both teaching and counseling, I became interested in the gifted student with a preference for sensing. As intuitive students can be "curriculum disabled" in a sensing classroom, so sensing students can feel mismatched with the traditionally intuitive perceiving curriculum of many gifted programs. The chess project discussed previously offers an example of a project which addresses this concern.

There are several classroom situations that highlight Sensing–Intuitive differences among students. One is the aversion to brain-storming alluded to previously. If anyone seems anxious about brain-storming, I ask her or him to come up with three ideas and three only; often, one ends up "allowing" newly enthusiastic sensing students to share a few more. Another focal situation is research using an encyclopedia: with intuitive students, the browse factor takes over as they exclaim over all the entries anywhere near the one they're looking for (what was it, anyway?). Once they've located their entry, however, they often can quickly pull out the main idea. The sensing student, on the other hand, usually goes right to the target entry, but often copies out every word, struggling with both skimming and recognizing the central ideas and themes.

Another concern is the widespread strategy of taking away free or recess time either to finish deskwork or as a punishment. A meaningful break is essential for restoration during the school day: the intuitive perceiving child is longing for unscheduled time; the extraverted individual is living to talk with friends; the sensing perceiving student and many others are ready for some physical activity; the child with a thinking preference may be looking forward to scripting an elaborate fantasy game that has been going on for weeks; the introverted young person will connect with the good friend she only sees at the break. . . . All of these children will return to the classroom more ready to settle into the school routine for the rest of the day. It's a dilemma for teachers because of the quantity of work to be covered, but it's often preferable to "compact" work in areas the student has mastered to free up class time or send work home, alerting parents that it's coming. Another problem with keeping students in the classroom over recess is that the teacher may miss her or his "free time" as well—time needed for at least as many reasons as there are types of teachers.

The elementary school population, including the teachers, overwhelmingly expresses a Feeling preference.[30] The adult pattern for the Thinking preference begins to emerge more clearly in middle school. The elementary school culture is thus usually a Feeling culture, and one imagines that the young students with a preference for Thinking[31] can feel at odds. One kindergarten boy, for example, told me that his teacher had never explained why she used phonetic spelling[32] and that he thought she did not know how to spell correctly until his mother explained the reasoning behind the method. His teacher had thought he was being critical of her, but in reality, he had been severely disappointed as he had anticipated learning at school for a long time. Such a child can become alienated long before he or she finds an academic fit in middle or high school.

A first-grade girl with a preference for Intuitive Thinking was captivated with the concept of infinity when she came up with the notion that if line segments were divided lengthwise, they could go on forever. Her well-meaning teacher, who had a more concrete approach to mathematics, told her she was wrong. This is a child who could have been mentored by a mathematician to nurture her curiosity and creativity. Are we losing potentially creative mathematicians and scientists in these early encounters with young thinking types? This is an area in which consultation with diverse colleagues can enrich the whole community. Perhaps an understanding of type can be a vehicle for creating a more welcoming environment for a range of intellectual styles. It is a worthwhile and rewarding effort. One second-grade teacher cultivated a small group of mathematically-inclined intuitive thinking students, beginning with calculating the cost of meals, tax and tips from local restaurant menus and culminating in letting them work with another teacher/mentor to develop and enact a business plan to get a small bank loan and start a company selling school pencils. At least two of those fortunate students are currently majoring in economics in college.

> As I have suggested, "normality" is a word capable
> of interpretation, meaning to some people the existing
> state of affairs while to me it means the potential which
> the existing state of affairs too often deforms. All children
> are gifted…
>
> Yehudi Menuhin[33]

Many students enjoy studying the ideas of psychological type itself, which offers one way to organize information they are already attuned to. One eight-year-old told me that "Now I know why people get mad at me. They aren't bothered because I know everything; they get mad because I'm an extravert and I have to *tell* everything I know." Another second-grader said that the talking feather (our talking stick in the *Tales*) was something introverts made up so that they could get some attention; he became perceptibly more tolerant as we conversed about why that might be.

There are many sources of type information and ideas in educational settings, among them the writings of Elizabeth Murphy and Gordon and Carolyn Lawrence. In *The Developing Child*,[34] Murphy writes specifically about ideas applicable to the classroom.

Chapter 6
Some Notes on Counseling

When I work with children, I often discuss type with them and give them a type measure, either the Murphy-Meisgeier Type Indicator for Children or the Myers-Briggs Type Indicator, depending on their ages. If possible, I send the MBTI home for the parents and siblings to complete, and invite the parents for a discussion of their family type picture. Such time together can be invaluable; family members often refer back to it, sometimes years later. I bring in written materials for the parents to take home, including copies of the feedback sheets for each family member. This is particularly important for sensing and introverted individuals who enjoy having reference materials as they reflect on the meeting.

Often, issues surface between the parents that can be discussed and reframed with type as a non-judgmental point of reference. For example, Intuitive-Sensing or Thinking-Feeling differences might be the source of disagreement about discipline or fundamental issues of family culture such as education and vacation planning. When these matters are discussed in the context of type, the conversation can focus on different strengths individuals bring to the family and ways those strengths can be honored to everyone's benefit. Often, parents remember that the differences giving them so much trouble now are the very qualities that first drew them to one another. They can begin to see how those dynamics, positive and negative, are being lived out with the children.

As mentioned earlier, children who are raised "against type" are in a difficult situation; they are not in a family culture that models or affirms their strengths. They exert enormous effort towards accommodating and inadvertently away from development of their natural ways of learning, valuing, deciding and acting. Sometimes a counselor is the first adult to become aware of the situation and can begin to open it up for discussion. Children usually welcome such discussion with relief as it brings a palpable discomfort into focus and understanding, and substantiates their own neglected preferences as real and of value. A kind of "falsification of type" can happen at the cultural, family or school level. It's a poignant situation to see and a rewarding one to identify as the huddled "ugly duckling" begins to stretch and claim a place among its fellow swans.

The MMTIC is a valuable and intriguing measure. I have used it with large groups of children, and also find it valuable one-on-one. The thoughtful items often generate rich conversations: for example, one item asks what you do if your overweight friend is not chosen for a team. Children with a strong Feeling preference may put a hand on their chest and say, "You make something up, but then it's wrong to lie. . . ." They are conflicted, but the deep value of not hurting feelings is evident. Thinking children often say, "You tell him because it's true. You don't want to hurt his feelings, but then at least he can do something about it..." They are also struggling, but find the moral dilemma a bit clearer. I like scoring the test with children, giving them direct feedback and ownership of the results. It's an opportunity to discuss type theory with even primary-aged children and support their developing preferences.

One reason for keeping this process—and others—open is that so many children we see have concerns around boundaries. I try to convey in as many ways possible that they have wisdom within, that they are the experts on themselves. Their ownership of experience, be it testing, drawing, thinking about how they like to learn or what they will contribute to the play in the instance described earlier, is deeply engaging.

We touched on some type and gender issues in previous discussion. While the data have changed or become broader in the other dimensions over time, the Thinking–Feeling sex difference has held. The difference is significant but not drastic: about 65% of women prefer Feeling and 35%, Thinking; the opposite obtains for males. Those who don't fit the prevailing stereotypes are in a numerous minority. It is valuable to refer back to Jung's notes on feeling and thinking as equal-but-different cognitive styles, as explored briefly in the introduction. As in other areas, the goal is to develop a strength as well as to cultivate its counterpart. The Thinking individual is at her best when tempered with her compassion, and the Feeling individual is most powerful when he is supported by his logic.

There is beginning to be some consideration of type and Attention Deficit/Hyperactivity Disorder in the type literature. This is an important area for research. My observation is that impulsive speaking and acting out may be particularly distressing to the introverted child who then has to cope with humiliation as others notice this involuntary behavior. Linda Silverman notes that it is possible that introverts may be good candidates for outgrowing ADHD as they mature.

Many counselors, teachers and parents are concerned with the apparently increasing numbers of students identified as ADHD. Each case requires serious scrutiny, looking at the individual, biological components and how environments might be tempered to enhance development. Some of the young people mentioned earlier had been designated ADHD when it seemed possible that their behavior was precipitated—at least in part—by being in family and academic situations particularly at odds with their gifts. Their "cries for help" had been labeled and in some cases medicated before the situation had been thoroughly explored.

Although a discussion of the shadow is not central to this book, it is an area worthy of further consideration. The shadow is what Naomi Quenk calls the "hidden personality" and is less conscious and evident than the manifest type of an individual. We discuss ways to work with the preferences and strengths of a child, but being attuned to the opposite dimensions is also enlightening. As logic and fairness can facilitate learning in a child with a preference for Thinking, so an appeal to Feeling can sometimes bring out a remarkably negative reaction in the same child. In her glossary, Quenk defines the shadow:

> "In Jungian psychology, the negative, unacceptable part of the psyche, characteristically a major part of the personal unconscious, it is the repository of all those things a person does not wish to acknowledge about him or herself. It often provides for content expressed when the inferior function has been constellated."[35]

There are many fine explorations of this topic: among them, Quenk's *Beside Ourselves: Our Hidden Personality in Everyday Life* and Maria Von Franz's *Jung's Typology: The Inferior Function.*

In the *Type Tales*, Millie's annoyance over Momo's trying to comfort the goalie is perhaps more than lack of understanding. It could also be influenced by her shadow connection with her own Feeling function, which might be experienced as undeveloped and chaotic, a frightening place. By the same token, Momo's hurt feelings when Millie doesn't offer the same overt approval he does could be more than just his lack of understanding of the Thinking way. It could be that he experiences an uncomfortable chill around his less preferred Thinking function.

Counselors may enjoy Jung's original writings in *Psychological Type*. The work of Judy Provost from her longtime counseling experiences in a college setting is valuable. Her book, *Procrastination*, is helpful for work with underachieving students. Hendrix's *Giving the Love that Heals* is a fine resource for families working with listening skills and understanding family dynamics.

Understanding one's self in type terms is invaluable in sustaining this dialogue with young people.

Afterword

In the passage from which Isabel Briggs Myers gently took the title of her book, human differences are framed as gifts, each essential to community: "Having then gifts differing according to the grace that is given to us. . . ." (Romans 12:6).

We bring our gifts in trust to the talking stick circle, wondering whether our unwieldy fragments of narrative might better be ignored, edited or hidden away for another time, a different circle. . . . But, as we settle into the moment, and the worn stick passes from hand to hand, our disparate tales begin to resonate in the deep rhythms of the story we create together.

At the beginning of this project, I proposed that the group portrait, Family Resemblance, be the cover. But I was convinced that Momo/Millie should welcome the reader. So, this exploration of diverse gifts concludes with a playful image to remind us that we share a family resemblance, that we are more alike than different, that we are in significant ways entrusted with the care of one another and our shared world.

References

Briggs Myers, Isabel, *Gifts Differing*. Palo Alto, CA: Consulting Psychologists Press, 1980(6).

Briggs Myers, Isabel, *Introduction to Type*. Palo Alto, CA: Consulting Psychologist Press, 1987(1962).

Briggs Myers, Isabel and McCaulley, Mary, *Manual: A Guide to the Development and Use of the Myers-Briggs Type Indicator*. Palo Alto, CA: Consulting Psychologists Press, 1985(1986).

Bruner, Jerome, *Actual Minds, Possible Worlds*. Cambridge, MA: Harvard University Press, 1986.

Buber, Martin, *I and Thou*. New York, NY: Charles Scribner's Sons, 1958.

Dinkmeir, Don and Losoncy, Lewis, *The Encouragement Book: Becoming a Positive Person*. New York, NY: Prentiss Hall Books, 1980.

Gilligan, Carol, *In A Different Voice: Psychological Theory and Women's Development*. Cambridge, MA: Harvard University Press, 1977.

Ginot, Haim, *Between Parent and Child, Between Parent and Teenager*. New York, NY: Avon, 1985.

Gordimer, Nadine, *Burger's Daughter*. New York, NY: Viking, 1979.

Hanson, J. Robert and Silver, Harvey F., *Teacher Self-Assessment*. Moosetown, NJ: Hanson Silver Associates, 1980.

Hendrix, Harville and Hunt, Helen, *Giving the Love that Heals: A Guide for Parents*. New York, NY: Pocket Books, 1997.

Jung, Carl, *Psychological Types*. Princeton, NJ: Princeton University Press, 1974. Bates translation was first published in 1923.

Kohlberg, Lawrence, *The Meaning and Measurement of Moral Development*. Massachusetts: Clark University, Heinz Weiner Institute, 1981.

Kroeger, Otto and Thueson, Janet, *Type Talk*. New York, NY: Delacorte Press, 1988.

Kurcinka, Mary Sheedy, *Raising Your Spirited Child*. New York, NY: Harper Collins, 1991.

Lawrence, Gordon, *People Types and Tiger Stripes*. Gainesville, FL: CAPT, 1993 (third edition).

McAdams, Dan P., Ph.D., *The Stories We Live By*. New York, NY: William Morrow and Co., 1993.

Martin, Charles, *Looking at Type™: The Fundamentals*. Gainesville, FL: CAPT, 1997.

McGee Cooper, Ann and Trammell, Duane, *Time Management for Unmanageable People*. New York, NY: Bantam Doubleday, 1994.

Meisgeier, Charles, and Murphy, Elizabeth, *The Murphy-Meisgeier Type Indicator for Children (MMTIC)*. Palo Alto, CA: Consulting Psychologists Press, 1987.

Menuhin, Yehudi, *Yehudi Menuhin: Unfinished Journey*. New York, NY, Knopf, 1977.

Murphy, Elizabeth, *I Am a Good Teacher*. Gainesville, FL: CAPT, 1987.

Murphy, Elizabeth, *The Developing Child: Using Jungian Type to Understand Children*. Gainesville, FL: CAPT, 1992.

Provost, Judy, *Applications of the Myers-Briggs Type Indicator in Counseling: A Casebook*. Gainesville, FL: CAPT, 1984.

Provost, Judy, *Procrastination: Using Psychological Types to Help Students*. Gainesville, FL: CAPT, 1988.

Polkinghorn, Donald E., *Narrative Knowing and the Human Sciences*. Albany, NY: State University Press of New York Press, 1988.

Quenk, Naomi, *Beside Ourselves: Our Hidden Personality in Everyday Life*. Palo Alto, CA: Consulting Psychologist Press, 1994.

Silverman, Linda, *Counseling the Gifted and Talented*. Denver, CO: Love, 1993.

Silverman, Linda, "Parenting Young Gifted Children" in Whitmore (Ed.) *Intellectual Giftedness in Young Children*. New York, NY: The Haworth Press, 1986.

Silverman, Linda, "Personality Plus," *Understanding Our Gifted*, November, 1988.

Silverstein, Olga, *The Courage to Raise Good Men*. New York, NY: Viking, 1994.

Wickes, Frances G., *The Inner World of Childhood*. Boston, MA: Sigo Press, 1988 (orig. 1927).

Williams, Rosalind, "Personality characteristics of gifted and talented students as measured by the MBTI and the MMTIC," Doctoral Dissertation, East Texas State University, 1992.

Vitz, Paul C., "The Use of Stories in Moral Development," *American Psychologist*, June 1990.

von Franz, Maria and Hillman, James, *Jung's Typology*. Chelsea, MI: Bookcrafters, 1971.

Zipkin, Amy, "The Teachings of Carl Jung," *New York Times Education Life*, November 7, 1999, pp. 21-23.

Footnotes

[1]McAdams, 1993

[2]Jung (1923) designated *thinking* and *feeling* the two rational functions and gave them equal weight. In an interesting parallel, Bruner (1986) distinguishes between the narrative and the paradigmatic mode of thinking and considers both powerful and discreetly different cognitive paths. Gilligan's (1977) work was part of a movement that honored and investigated narrative and contextual knowing, challenging Kohlberg's (1981) hierarchical model of moral development. Polkinghorn (1988) explored the use of a narrative rather than a traditional scientific model to revitalize social science research.

[3]Polkinghorn, 1988, p. 1

[4]Buber, Martin, 1958, p. 11

[5]Jung, 1923

[6]Jung, 1974(23), p. 330

[7]Jung, 1974(23), p. 331

[8]von Franz, 1971, p. 3

[9]Myers, Isabel Briggs, 1986 (80), p. 200

[10]von Franz and Hillman, 1971

[11]Should a dominant not emerge for various reasons, the individual could fail to reach her/his potential. See von Franz, 1971. Also, Jung, 1974(23), p. 332

[12]as quoted in Gordimer, 1979, p. 213

[13]*The Manual: A Guide to the Development and Use of the Myers-Briggs Type Indicator* by Myers and McCaulley, 1985, *Type Talk* by Kroeger and Thuesen, 1988 and *Looking at Type™: the Fundamentals* by Charles Martin, 1997

[14]Myers, Isabel Briggs, 1986, pp. 181-2

[15]Murphy, 1992, p. 55

[16]Kroeger, Otto and Thuesen, Janet, Type Talk, New York, Dell, 1988, p. 265

[17]Kroeger, Otto and Thuesen, Janet, 1988, p. 238

[18]Myers, 1980

[19]Martin, 1997, p. 49

[20]Myers, 1980, p. 196

[21]Hendrix, 1997

[22]Ginot, 1985

[23]Silverman, 1986

[24]Myers, p. 152-3

[25]Murphy, 1992, pp. 79-81

[26]Murphy, 1987

[27]Wickes, 1927, p. 134

[28]Silverman, (1988, p. 11) indicates that about 60% of gifted are introverts while about 25% of the general population expresses this preference. However, Williams (1992) found extraverts overly represented in a gifted/talented sample.

[29]Silverman, 1986

[30]Martin, 1997, p. 50. Moving towards college, educators are increasingly intuitive thinking, though the data presents a more complex pattern than is discussed here.

[31]Murphy and Meisgeier found that 80% of elementary age girls and 67% of the boys preferred Feeling, so this dimension must have a strong developmental component as 35% of adult women and 65% of adult men express a Thinking preference.

[32]Why isn't "phonetic" spelled "fonetic"...?

[33]Menuhin, 1977

[34]Murphy, 1992

[35]Quenk, 1993, p. 279

Appendix

The following appendix, *Effects of the Combinations of all Four Preferences in Young People* was reproduced by special permission of the Publisher, Consulting Psychologist Press, Inc., Palo Alto, CA 94306 from *Introduction to Type* by Isabel Briggs Myers © 1980. Further reproduction is prohibited without the Publisher's consent.

Effects of the Combinations of All

SENSING TYPES

	WITH THINKING	**WITH FEELING**
INTROVERTS — **JUDGING**	### ISTJ Serious, quiet, earn success by concentration and thoroughness. Practical, orderly, matter-of-fact, logical, realistic and dependable. See to it that everything is well organized. Take responsibility. Make up their own minds as to what should be accomplished and work toward it steadily, regardless of protests or distractions. Live their outer life more with thinking, inner more with sensing.	### ISFJ Quiet, friendly, responsible and conscientious. Work devotedly to meet their obligations and serve their friends and school. Thorough, painstaking, accurate. May need time to master technical subjects, as their interests are not often technical. Patient with detail and routine. Loyal, considerate, concerned with how other people feel. Live their outer life more with feeling, inner more with sensing.
INTROVERTS — **PERCEIVING**	### ISTP Cool onlookers, quiet, reserved, observing and analyzing life with detached curiosity and unexpected flashes of original humor. Usually interested in impersonal principles, cause and effect, or how and why mechanical things work. Exert themselves no more than they think necessary, because any waste of energy would be inefficient. Live their outer life more with sensing, inner more with thinking.	### ISFP Retiring, quietly friendly, sensitive, modest about their abilities. Shun disagreements, do not force their opinions or values on others. Usually do not care to lead but are often loyal followers. May be rather relaxed about assignments or getting things done, because they enjoy the present moment and do not want to spoil it by undue haste or exertion. Live their outer life more with sensing, inner more with feeling.
EXTRAVERTS — **PERCEIVING**	### ESTP Matter-of-fact, do not worry or hurry, enjoy whatever comes along. Tend to like mechanical things and sports, with friends on the side. May be a bit blunt or insensitive. Can do math or science when they see the need. Dislike long explanations. Are best with real things that can be worked, handled, taken apart or put back together. Live their outer life more with sensing, inner more with thinking.	### ESFP Outgoing, easygoing, accepting, friendly, fond of a good time. Like sports and making things. Know what's going on and join in eagerly. Find remembering facts easier than mastering theories. Are best in situations that need sound common sense and practical ability with people as well as with things. Live their outer life more with sensing, inner more with feeling.
EXTRAVERTS — **JUDGING**	### ESTJ Practical realists, matter-of-fact with a natural head for business or mechanics. Not interested in subjects they see no use for, but can apply themselves when necessary. Like to organize and run activities. Tend to run things well, especially if they remember to consider other people's feelings and points of view when making their decisions. Live their outer life more with thinking, inner more with sensing.	### ESFJ Warm-hearted, talkative, popular, conscientious, born cooperators, active committee members. Always doing something nice for someone. Work best with plenty of encouragement and praise. Little interest in abstract thinking or technical subjects. Main interest is in things that directly and visibly affect people's lives. Live their outer life more with feeling, inner more with sensing.

Four Preferences in Young People

INTUITIVE TYPES

WITH FEELING

WITH THINKING

INFJ Succeed by perseverance, originality and desire to do whatever is needed or wanted. Put their best efforts into their work. Quietly forceful, conscientious, concerned for others. Respected for their firm principles. Likely to be honored and followed for their clear convictions as to how best to serve the common good. Live their outer life more with feeling, inner more with intuition.	**INTJ** Have original minds and great drive which they use only for their own purposes. In fields that appeal to them they have a fine power to organize a job and carry it through with or without help. Skeptical, critical, independent, determined, often stubborn. Must learn to yield less important points in order to win the most important. Live their outer life more with thinking, inner more with intuition.
INFP Full of enthusiasms and loyalties, but seldom talk of these until they know you well. Care about learning, ideas, language, and independent projects of their own. Apt to be on yearbook staff, perhaps as editor. Tend to undertake too much, then somehow get it done. Friendly, but often too absorbed in what they are doing to be sociable or notice much. Live their outer life more with intuition, inner more with feeling.	**INTP** Quiet, reserved, brilliant in exams, especially in theoretical or scientific subjects. Logical to the point of hair-splitting. Interested mainly in ideas, with little liking for parties or small talk. Tend to have very sharply defined interests. Need to choose careers where some strong interest of theirs can be used and useful. Live their outer life more with intuition, inner more with thinking.
ENFP Warmly enthusiastic, high-spirited, ingenious, imaginative. Able to do almost anything that interests them. Quick with a solution for any difficulty and ready to help anyone with a problem. Often rely on their ability to improvise instead of preparing in advance. Can always find compelling reasons for whatever they want. Live their outer life more with intuition, inner more with feeling.	**ENTP** Quick, ingenious, good at many things. Stimulating company, alert and outspoken, argue for fun on either side of a question. Resourceful in solving new and challenging problems, but may neglect routine assignments. Turn to one new interest after another. Can always find logical reasons for whatever they want. Live their outer life more with intuition, inner more with thinking.
ENFJ Responsive and responsible. Feel real concern for what others think and want, and try to handle things with due regard for other people's feelings. Can present a proposal or lead a group discussion with ease and tact. Sociable, popular, active in school affairs, but put time enough on their studies to do good work. Live their outer life more with feeling, inner more with intuition.	**ENTJ** Hearty, frank, able in studies, leaders in activities. Usually good in anything that requires reasoning and intelligent talk, such as public speaking. Are well-informed and keep adding to their fund of knowledge. May sometimes be more positive and confident than their experience in an area warrants. Live their outer life more with thinking, inner more with intuition.

INTROVERTS — JUDGING / PERCEIVING

EXTRAVERTS — PERCEIVING / JUDGING